even

DOROTHY CROSS

ARNOLFINI
BRISTOL

foreword

even is an exhibition of new work made by the artist Dorothy Cross between 1994 and 1996. New developments in the work focus upon confusing accepted patterns of inheritance and exploring notions of authority. The artist combines and disrupts objects which have a resonance of their past life and are evocative of personal memory or family history. These works involve both found and made objects in conjunction with organic matter such as snakes and cows' udders. The artist has based herself in Dublin for more than ten years after studying and working abroad. As one of a number of internationally known artists from Ireland, Arnolfini is delighted to be able to show her most recent body of work which after Bristol will tour to Ikon Gallery, Birmingham and Oriel Mostyn, Llandudno. At the end of the year a selection of work will be shown at Frith Street Gallery, London.

Tessa Jackson and **Josephine Lanyon**
Arnolfini

even
adverb
    used to emphasise a comparison – to greater degree
    used to suggest that something mentioned is unlikely or is an extreme case or should be compared
    with what might have happened
adjective
    level, free from irregularities
    uniform in quality
    calm
    equally balanced

earlier work

The word *even* can suggest a sense of balance between two parts or elements which are matched in some way. One meaning of *even* which this exhibition aims to present is the re-balancing of the perception of Dorothy Cross's work. Indeed this show comes at a time when the artist is ready to present a recent body of work made over the last eighteen months to two years. The works are a synthesis of earlier preoccupations and new stimuli, underwritten by long-term enquiries into the nature of sexuality and what constitutes the female and the feminine. By implication maleness and masculinity provides a corollary throughout.

After being included in a number of shows such as *Bad Girls* in 1994 and *Fetishism* in 1995 which attracted spirited media and cultural comment, Cross was seen and acclaimed as an artist, by her udder works. They seemed to eclipse her earlier work. In many ways the reaction to her use of this biological item – sometimes disturbing, sometimes humorous and always intellectually and physically arresting meant her work became emblemised and thus easily mis-represented. In fact *even* brings to a close the udder works with *Pointing the Finger* and *Trunk*, in which the latter forms the culmination of this body of work made between 1992 to 1995. However, the spirit of earlier work, made after her return from America in 1983, through to pieces created in the Power House in 1990-91, is apparent in her most recent work. Throughout the entire period she continued to use objects which have their own story and sense of history. She continued to embrace surrealism by the fact that the objects have become dislodged in time and place and are now associated with the artist's and viewer's own unconscious imaginings. She has continued to juxtapose found objects and images in a series of pieces which read figuratively, creating metaphors and allegories linking the known and familiar, with the unknown and unconscious. Dorothy Cross continues to enjoy the materiality of her objects and the use of different media as she adjoins existing function and integrity with new materials, bringing forth fresh associations and readings.

In her exhibition entitled *Ebb* at The Douglas Hyde Gallery, Dublin in 1988 the artist showed works dating from 1985 which have no overriding theme either in the use of materials or subject matter. They all possess further meaning outside their sculptural form and are unified only in the language which Cross invents for herself. Some are installation based such as *Mother*, where the positioning of a tin bath, a large light bulb, two tea sieves and a fabricated wooden arch, which supports a plank of wood balanced out over the bath like a springboard at a swimming pool, is precise. Others are self contained such as *Erotic Couple* where two wooden towers are juxtaposed – one erect with a steel hoop as a head and a light bulb protruding from its middle, the other flopped over and split from base to midway like legs and crowned with brass wire for hair, which touches the floor as it arches backwards. In all these works there is no certainty of reading – in *Erotic Couple* the brass wire could equally symbolise a spent force after ejaculation through the steel hoop, or a feminine figure aroused by the penile light bulb. The boundaries between the sexes are unclear, each form could take the charateristics of female or male. It is this very conjunction of uncertainty and unconscious which excites the artist and allows the viewer to bring their own experience to bear.

In another major show entitled *Power House* work made from 1989 to 1991 was brought together. These works that were re-installed at the Intitute of Contemporary Art, University of Pennsylvania, came originally from an abandoned electricity generating station which is the major visual and physical feature of Dublin Bay. Once, in its omnipotence it supplied all the electricity to the capital of Ireland. Cross rented part of it as a work place and set up studio in the Pump House. In this decaying edifice of power and strength her work juxtaposed the industrial with the domestic. She used objects she found lying around, incorporating them into her own questioning of society and letting them live out their own histories again. *Parthenon* (also seen at Camden Arts Centre) as a structure, utilised found wooden lockers which still bore pictures pinned up or clothes and shoes abandoned by workmen long gone. The viewer was invited to peer through peep holes in the doors into a small space containing a bed. The superstructure of the bed was suggested by a working of wire mesh – revealing amongst its structure, the form of a phallus twisted into the skeletal mattress. Is this a form of female fetishism, or is it a symbol of emasculated power? Another work in the same exhibition provided a powerful gender juxtaposition. Entitled *Screen (Ladies Changing Room)*, the viewer looked through more peep holes to a bench with hooks above on which hung a row of cast-bronze hard hats. The screen has the feel and colour of the previous locker room doors, the hard hats faithful in every detail except at their top they are finished with a nipple. The colloquial 'wearing of hats' takes on fresh meaning if gender can be changed that easily. The empty changing room bench suggests both presence and absence – who or what uses the space or the hats? The reality of the construction hat crowned with an aroused nipple possesses complete ambiguity.

The udder works continue to develop the meanings of these earlier pieces although their physicality almost eclipsed them. The use of the cow's udder suggested itself to the artist after a visit to Norway in early 1990. Invited to make a site visit for the Artscape Nordland Project she discovered a cow's udder in the form of a domestic sieve hanging on the back of a door in a local museum. Stretched across a wooden rim, the udder possessed irregular handmade perforations. Cross was captivated by the fact that a cow could be used for purposes other than nourishment. In medieval times the udder itself was eaten, with even Samuel Pepys recording in his diary "where he and I and my Will had a good udder to dinner".[1] The word 'uddered' was frequently used to described something as being drawn dry.

From 1992 a very productive period followed where Cross moved easily from work to work, employing some

---

1   Samuel Pepys, *Diaries*, date unknown

Virgin Shroud 1993

part of the udder each time. On occasion the udder with its four teats would be incorporated, at other times a single teat would be used. As nature's symbol of the mother, this most familiar domestic animal that goes by a name which is also given to the female side of other species became a leit motif. Throughout mythology the character and image of the cow denotes goodness, dependability, domesticity and maternal qualities. It can also be used as a denigratory term, implying stupidity or docility. The udder with its own identification of nurturing and suckling immediately opens up the parallels with the breast. Freud was convinced that "the mother's breast is the starting point of the whole sexual life, the un-matched prototype of every later sexual satisfaction to which fantasy often recurs in times of need".[2] Many of the udders once they have been worked with, no longer give the feeling of comfort, they disrupt convention and the associations of providing milk are destroyed.

Virgin Shroud of 1993 is one of the most monumental of the udder pieces. On top of the head appear teats, and then cascading down falls cow hide lined with her grandmother's wedding train from 1914. No specific reference is made to the body, no human anatomy can be seen. It is the very opposite of the half clad figure in classical art where the chiton falls loosely from the female shoulders often emphasing the breast and the curvacious form beneath. The Greek tunic even gave sight of feet peeping out from underneath, completing a heroine type form. Instead *Virgin Shroud* emphasises impregnability, it forms a protective covering and hides any reference to sexual

2 *The Complete Psychological Works of Sigmund Freud*, Standard Editiion, XVI p.314, London, 1953

identity as well as obliterating the intellect. It might in shape resemble the form of the Virgin Mary. Strangely the giving of milk was one of the few biological functions the Mother of God could perform, and was often shown doing so in pictoral references. As such this gave her the symbolism of life and sustinance of the Christian soul. Yet here *Virgin Shroud* looks immoveable and without compassion and contains no symbol of motherhood.

In another memorable work *Amazon* presents a dressmaker's dummy covered in cow hide, with its udder and one teat forming a single breast in the centre of the chest. This reference to the Greek warrior women who followed Artemis, hunting and denying themselves relationships with men, turns the animal teat into a firm and erect breast. Usually the breast is the most vulnerable part of the female body but the Amazons by cutting off one breast in order to hunt with their bows and arrows better, mutilated themselves and created a single enhanced sexual organ. Seen as lying outside the limits of civilisation, the Amazons have become symbols of independence and strength, in part due to their virginal image. Simultaneously in other images of women the single revealed breast denoted Charity. "In Greek, the root *mamm*-e gives both the word for breast, the word for a child's cry for the breast, and the name of mother, as it still does in English, and the Romance languages. In Greek literature, the revealed breast often designates the claim of a mother's love upon a hero, the bond that still joins the private and the public worlds."[3] Here the duality of the breast as original sustainer of a child's life is set against its use as a symbol of erotic invitation. The title of the work might also refer to uncharted territory or territory so dense as to render it almost impassable. This carries with it a similar feel to that of the Virgin Shroud and plays upon the notion of Amazon women as untouchable and uncharted by men.

In both *Virgin Shroud* and *Amazon* the female figure has no individual identity. As with other female figures Pandora, Eve and Helen of Troy, "their stories express an understanding that they bear meanings ascribed to them by their creators, that their identity is perceived through the eyes of others, not their own."[4] Marina Warner suggests that "the female form tends to symbolic interpretation, the male resists anonymous universality robustly, and often manages to retain individuality even while calling higher things to mind."[5] Mythologically the male was always seen as the intellect. As a result the female form lost all personality. In both these pieces Cross has maintained this historical convention, yet she ensures that the works possess a statuesque gravitas which cannot be dismissed.

Pandora is simultaneously the prototype for the attractive female and the evil enchantress. The udder and the teat likewise move from the soft comforter to the hardened (particularly when dry) phallic like form. In a number of works Cross made at this time, such as *Stool* covered with a stretched udder and *Saddle* or *Vaulting Horse* when in each case the recognised object is rendered dysfunctional, there is a disturbing thought that they may form objects of self arousal. *Trunk* takes this to its conclusion, where teat becomes penis (see Marian Dunlea's text). In these instances elements of the work question what constitutes the female or the male. Differentness is contained in the psyche rather than the physical, sexuality is expressed as representation.

Among these works, some exist which are more modest in size and reading. Several are counterbalanced by

3 Marina Warner, *Monuments and Maidens*, p.282, Vintage, 1996 (first published George Weidenfeld and Nicolson Ltd., 1985)
4 *Ibid.*, p.224
5 *Ibid.*, p.225

the humour they arouse. The single teat tied over the mouth of a Guinness bottle or the udder and teats which coat a rugby ball – give immediate readings. Does alchohol nurture us all? Hardened teats on the outside of the ball render it inappropriate to play with or in the case of *Croquet* where all the balls are covered, they are entirely unusable. The two former create images connected to male needs and the male domain – the penile teats become absurd. A pair of stiletto shoes with teats for pointed toes are reminiscent of Meret Oppenheim and have the same serenity and beauty which is absent in some of the udder works. The udder or teats' presence sometimes promote a reaction of disgust – for example the teat at the centre of a dart board acting as bull's eye. This part of the cow has been de-animalised, it has been severed from its usual associations. Returning to the sieve on the back of the museum door brings the realisation of how far Cross has taken this item we usually think little about.

The Sieve of Tuccia in the National Gallery, London by Giovanni Battista Moroni is one example of the use of the sieve as an allegory of virtue or chastity. Tuccia holds it on her right knee, but it is shown half full of water although the collander as you would expect has perforations. Defying nature the sieve was occasionally used in early religious art and as Marina Warner reminds us "it comes as near to a perfect instrument of disclosure about the nature of the virtuous female body as any imaginative *figura* can. The inviolability of the allegorical figure, portrayed as a sealed container of the meaning she conveys, helped differentiate her sphere from the individual female's, who belongs to time and flux and is subject to change."[6] Like many artists before her Cross has taken the sieve, in this a case cow's udder, as an allegorical emblem and exposed it, through juxtaposition, and given it many figurative and metaphorical readings. As an object it oscillates between its own characteristics and objectivity, and that of otherness.

Object

It must have been an odd object to begin with.
Now the ghosts of its uses
Whisper around my head, tickle the tips
Of my fingers. Weeds
Reclaim with quick silence the beams, pillars
Doorways. Places change, and a small object
Stands defiant in its placelessness.
Durable because it contains intensely meanings
Which it can no longer pour out.
Jimmie Durham, 1964[7]

Tessa Jackson
Director, Arnolfini

---

6   *Ibid.*, p242
7   Quoted from Laura Mulvey, *Fetishism amd Curiosity*, p175, British Film Institute, 1996 (first published in *Jimmie Durham*, Phaidon Press 1964)

Amazon 1992

even DOROTHY CROSS

On the face of it, Dorothy Cross's work is anything but even. Characteristically, it amalgamates found and constructed objects, but that is about as much as you can say for it in terms of a signature style. You might intimate that some of the constructed items have about them the hallmarks of manufactured ready-mades but, just to confuse matters, the forms themselves are frequently biomorphic. If we are truly endeavouring to seek within her sculpture an index of uniformity perhaps heterogeneity is the most appropriate parameter at our disposal.

Cross's singular approach to making art means that her constructed assemblages invariably have the effect of reinvigorating the lives of everyday objects. The artist originally trained in three-dimensional design and jewellery and admits to taking delight in the more material aspects of her sculpture, a disclosure which finds palpable form in *Iris*, *Cuttlefish Rings* and *Rings*. "The majority of the found things which I use in my work actually belonged to my family," Cross acknowledges. "I grew up with these things and for me they have an immense history. By making them into art, I get rid of them. I feel that I am passing them away from me. I have inherited all these things, but in using them in this way I am breaking the line of inheritance."[1]

A number of commentators have suggested that the artist's work evinces a uniform patina of usage and time.[2] This aspect allows it to shuttle back and forth so that sometimes individual pieces appear archaic and at other times thoroughly modern. Although this is not a quality which Cross actively seeks to impart to her work, she is happy with the correspondences which it generates. "I don't try to fake age, but evidence of use is something I like enormously. Good art should make you consider yourself in relation to time, which means in relation to birth, life and death. The Japanese have a word for rust which evokes the life that a thing has lived, its pre-existing and continuing history."

As with so much of her sculpture, the sixteen separate pieces which are being shown together in the current exhibition set themselves the task of questioning representations of control and desire. Like *Goggles*, they do this by commenting on the dynamics of masculinity and femininity. In an earlier essay on Cross, John Hutchinson described the formulation of gender as a psychic construction rather than a form of immutable psychological

---

1   All quotations by the artist are from an unpublished discussion with the author which took place in the artist's Dublin home in January 1996
2   Most notably Melissa Feldman in 'Power Plays', *Power House*, Institute of Contemporary Arts, Philadelphia, 1991

13

difference, but just as much as Cross's work makes reference to the dichotomy between and continuity of maleness and femaleness, so it contrasts the real with the imagined, the natural with the synthetic and the public with the private.[3] In some instances in the past, the combinations have been even more specific, juxtaposing the domestic with the industrial and the fish-like with the mammalian. These other references are less forceful in the ways in which they solicit our attention, but are no less profound in what they reveal about the organic and inorganic worlds in which we operate and show that Cross has always addressed her art to agendas outside those which might be regarded as exclusively anthropocentric.

Sometimes, as in *Croquet*, Cross's interest in dualities has been delineated within the same piece. On other occasions, best exemplified by the couples in *Ebb* 1998, they have surfaced in an alliance between separate sculptures. These depictions of twofoldedness speak of possibility rather than probability and of fragmentation rather than single truths and imply that Cross is just as confused as the rest of us when it comes to arriving at a better understanding of selfhood through an examination of her place in the world. "Unless you are a propagandist then it isn't really possible to make a piece of work which will only be read in one way. I am interested in a resistance to authority, whether that's about appreciation or information."

Cross's work was first seen in Britain in 1984 in a group exhibition entitled *Sculpture in the Chair*, but her

3 John Hutchinson in 'Cross' Purposes', *Artforum*, May 1993

largest one-person show prior to *even*, was *Parthenon* at Camden Arts Centre in London in 1992. *Parthenon* was first exhibited at the Institute of Contemporary Art in Philadelphia in 1991 as part of a larger installation entitled *Power House*. That installation recreated within the shell of an art gallery the topography of and meanings contained in the artist's old Dublin studio, a disused electricity-generating station whose rooms and corridors oozed memories of a quintessentially masculine environment. The locker-clad precinct of *Parthenon* had doors left ajar and was breached at various points with drill holes. These allowed the viewer to glimpse the personal effects that had once belonged to the workmen and other constructed objects – be-nippled hard-hats and a bed incorporating within its frame a woven phallus – whilst simultaneously limiting the ability of him or her to physically intervene in the space.

With *Parthenon*, drilling was a functional expedient, but the use of the drill carries far greater symbolic value in a new work called *Bible*. The bible in question, a large, old leather-bound edition, is displayed open at a spread featuring the two Marys at the Sepulchre together with one other unidentified female. To those for whom books represent the possibility of knowledge and the potential for truth, drilling appears to be an act of mindless violence, but Cross is keen to disabuse the viewer of this notion. "For Christians," she says, "the bible represents the point at which word and spirit come together. For me, by working with it, this bible has become a personal icon. In a fetishistic way I have made a precious object from something close to hand."

Inadvertently, the perforation which pierces *Bible* partially deletes the breasts of the Marys and, more poignantly, their hearts. Its presence passes comment on many aspects of christianity. The bible in question was given to the artist by her mother and spent a long time in the studio before Cross made up her mind what to do with it. "Suddenly," she declares, "I just had this image of the bible with a hole. It's very pleasurable to drill a perfect hole. As a child, I used to spend hours with a compass trying to draw a perfect circle so that you had no idea where the pencil line met. When I drilled the bible, my mother asked me, 'Why have you done this?' To begin with, I didn't know, but the decision to have the bible open at the page where the two Marys visit the Sepulchre and find it empty made me realise why. The body of Jesus has gone and that's the point in the bible where corporeality is removed permanently. Drilling the hole was an attempt to reinvest the bible with physicality. To me the bible creates a negative energy. It's full of wonderful stories, the messages of which are inherently good, but it also harbours some of the most destructive information. My reaction to that isn't to take a hatchet to it or burn it, but to pierce it with a very controlled void. It's still possible to read most of it, but by removing the slight linkages between one line and the next it completely unravels."

The titles which Cross gives her works allow them a narrative thrust which locks them fixedly into their formal, social, political and cultural contexts. Simultaneously, the unsettling nature of the imagery ensures that her art continues to operate in a fantastic realm presided over by belief and myth. The sculptures' meanings are frequently hermetic and occasionally appear open to interpretation only by a close group of initiates, an attribute which generates associations with Surrealism. Like the Surrealists, Cross seems to be engaged in a species of alchemy whose residue threatens the integrity of our social, sexual and animal identities. The ideas transmitted by and the materials used in the work are never less than challenging and more often than not induce in her audience an overwhelming sense of discomfiture. Cross does not set out with any programmatic intention to agitate yet she fully acknowledges her desire to disconcert. "A certain amount of discomfort prevents passivity. I detest complacency. I try to create discomfort for myself, too, by putting together things from my past, which I'm comfortable with, with things that are unfamiliar and peculiar."

Of all the materials with which she works, it is with the cow's udder that Cross has become most closely linked. The artist first made use of the organ by humorously placing it at the head-end of a *Vaulting Horse* in 1992. Since then, she has employed udders on numerous occasions, either as a stand-in for the head or as a covering over a variety of easily recognisable forms. While visiting Norway in the early 1990s Cross stumbled upon a sieve in a local museum which had been fabricated out of a stretched cow's udder. The effect on her was immediate. "It was the most exciting thing I had come across since Meret Oppenheim's *Fur Teacup*. Seeing that a cow could be used for something other than just producing milk was a total revelation. Using udders makes me feel like a cross between a butcher and a scientist. The whole process generates a strange mixture of disgust, hilarity and excitement. It wasn't until later that I remembered that Freud had spoken about the symbolism of cows' udders in Dora's case history."

In his Case Histories, Freud attempts to explain the cause of hysteria in a patient known as Dora.[4] Dora had never broken herself of the habit of sucking and retained a memory of her childhood in which she saw herself sucking at her nurse's breast and at the same time pulling rhythmically at the lobe of her nurse's ear. The mucous membrane of the lips and mouth is a primary erotogenic zone and intense activity of this at an early age is thought to determine the subsequent presence of a somatic compliance – the physical factor which governs the site of a neurotic symptom – on the part of the tract of tissue which begins at the lips. "Thus," says Freud, "at a time when the sexual object proper, that is, the male organ, has already become known, circumstances may arise which once more increase the excitation of the oral zone whose erotogenic character has been retained. It then needs very little creative power to substitute the sexual object of the moment (the penis) for the original object (the nipple) or for the finger which does duty for it." In concluding Dora's case history, Freud infers that "in most instances a cow's udder has aptly played the part of an image intermediate between a nipple and a penis."

When it comes to psychoanalysis, Cross finds herself more in sympathy with Jung than Freud. Jungian analysis encourages multiple readings of a situation whereas Freudian analysis only allows for a singular interpretation. "My work has been described as anxious-making," relates Cross, "but maybe that sounds too neurotic. I think confusion is what it's about. Aren't we always full of confusion? Even if you love somebody one day, you are bewildered the next. One day you're happy, the next you're unhappy."

Provoked by Freud, the Surrealists made a virtue out of fetishism and Cross uses the term herself to describe her own work. The udder-based work, including *Pointing the Finger*, is marked by a compulsive property

---

4   "Fragment of an analysis of a case of hysteria (Dora)", *Case Histories*, Sigmund Freud, Penguin Books, London, 1987

Pointing the Finger 1994

which embraces seduction and repulsion, pleasure and pain in equal part, and reflects an interest in confronting taboos and accessing their potency for transformation. The three images which make up the photographic triptych *Pointing the Finger* depict the artist's finger in a cow's teat variously hanging down, being held and being assertive. The artist was provoked into performing with a teat by a quotation which she came across which described the inside of a cow as the darkest place in the world.[5] "I dislike this identification of the female with the dark and the mysterious and the unknown. I would imagine being inside a cow is no darker than being inside a bull. It's not gender-specific. By putting my finger inside a cow's teat and using it in different ways, I'm truly getting inside it, confronting that sense of disapproval and contradicting the notion that females have to be docile and harmless and obedient."

The sexual charge in the udder-based work reaches a disturbing crescendo in *Trunk* which brings together, in the confined space of an old wooden chest, a pair of women's knickers with a cow's teat sewn into the gusset. It is more than thirty years since the mass availability of the contraceptive pill and legalisation of abortion made it possible for women to take control over their own bodies. In re-defining objects as subjects, the widespread acceptance of female sexuality in Western cultures has been a powerful force for good, but it is still regarded in some quarters with suspicion. The apprehension of female sexuality is probably at its most extreme in the context of the auto-erotic which brings with it for men the lurking, corrupting fear of a world without them. "There are few works that I've made which I have hidden," admits Cross, "but *Trunk* was one of them. When I finally finished the piece I thought, 'Oh God, what am I doing here? This is too weird.' But then weeks later, I began to understand it and decided to show it regardless of its reception. This is the first and probably last time that I will ever place a cow's teat genitally, but it had to be done."

Cross has chosen organic materials as the basis for much of her output and in doing so reflects a widespread distress about the body and self. "Some people get annoyed with my work because they think I'm being deliberately provocative, but I don't think I am. It's not in my nature to be like that. For me, art is an adventure that helps me cope with this ridiculous situation of being alive." It is a commonly held position that we manifest our concern about our relationship with the social body through our individual bodies. In dealing in *Trunk* with masturbation, the artist is not only asking her audience to contemplate the joys of self-stimulation, but to consider also the ways in which social and sexual inequalities lead to introspection and withdrawal.

The worlds which the artist calls forth are redolent of scenes from childhood when sensory experiences are at their most pronounced. Memories and visions are never again so vivid as they are when we are growing up, an observation reflected in the visionary and dream-like faces of the boys and girls who have been asked by Cross to *Close your eyes and open your mouth and see what God*. The trick-or-treat nature of the game, which might just as easily result in a mouthful of worms as a gobful of sweets, dwells on the trust, need and receptivity of youth and conjures up the innocence which most of us lose as adults.

---

5   W W Swett, *Dairy Husbandman*, US Department of Agriculture, 1947

The snake first made its appearance in Cross's work in *Irish Coronation Chair* of 1984. There the serpent was arranged in circular form suggestive of continuity, integration and regeneration and brought to mind Saint Patrick, generally credited with banishing all snakes from Ireland. In the pieces which Cross has recently been engaged with, the serpent has been arranged in linear fashion. The snake is one of the oldest allegorical symbols, a highly complex and universal form variously representing male, female and the self-created, death and destruction, resurrection and cycles of manifestation. It is solar and lunar, light and darkness, good and evil, wisdom and blind passion, healing and poison, preserver and destroyer and both spiritual and psychic rebirth. It is phallic and the presence of a serpent is almost universally associated with pregnancy. It accompanies, in world mythology, all female deities and is secret, enigmatic and intuitional. Two snakes together symbolise the opposites of dualism which are ultimately united and are therefore representative of healing. Seemingly hermaphrodite or sexless, snakes dominate proceedings in *Convention*, *Gallows*, *Bandaged Snake* and *Lover Snakes*.

In *Lover Snakes*, the passionate embrace of two serpents does nothing to reel in their reliqueried hearts, emotionally preserved at a safe distance from their respective bodies, sent there perhaps by disappointing pairings in the past. "The snake is a neutral thing sexually," says Cross, "in that it is very difficult to tell the male from the female. When I first began working with them I was tempted to sexualise and thereby differentiate them, but I have decided against that. More than anything else, I am interested in common mortality, common love and common struggle and the snake provides the perfect metaphor for that commonality. The *Lover Snakes* are about love and hope and protectiveness. They are very much together, these serpents, but they are also looking after their hearts." Shared experience is a theme which similarly lies at the centre of the two photographic images which reflect on the Crucifixion. In one of these the dead Christ à la Mantegna has been replaced with a female form. In the other the figure of Jesus has fallen away to leave a messy, androgynous outline.

In the 1980s, Cross tended to produce work which cohered in closely-related series, allowing the ideas from one sculpture to spill over into its relatives. The *Spires* of 1984-85 mixed church architecture with machinery and mechanically produced objects. From just before come the throne-like sculptures known as *Chairs* and both sets of work propose questions about Irish cultural identity. The couples of *Ebb* and subsequent work with udders and snakes show that Cross has continued to avail herself of a methodology which allows complex and polyvalent issues to be approached from a range of different positions. "With the udder-based pieces, I was trying to create a new reputation for the cow. Now I am trying to do the same thing for the down-trodden and misunderstood snake. As a symbol of temptation and betrayal, the snake has been systematically abused over time. It carries with it an abominable reputation. By executing it in *Gallows*, I wanted to make reference to that. Is it going up the scaffolding to sacrifice itself or has it been sentenced to death through misunderstanding."

Misunderstanding is powerfully represented in *Convention*. Here the snakes have been brought together in a circle and are attempting to communicate, but their speech bubbles are empty. The frustration and disempowerment which these reptiles encounter mirror the bafflement and inadequacy which we all sometimes experience as we make our idiosyncratic ways through life. *Bandaged Snake* shows that sometimes we get badly hurt as a consequence of these confusions. Away from the snake-based pieces, the 30-part photowork called *Rugby* reveals that some human acts which we assume to be aggressive are in part marked by great sensitivity and delicacy. *Kiss*, by contrast, shows that a moment of supreme human affection is visceral, ungainly and skeletal and the constant presence of death in life finds like-anatomical expression in the skilfully constructed head-and-baby montage which remains *Untitled*.

Although Dorothy Cross has chosen to portray in her work some of the more problematic aspects of life in general and the human condition in particular, there resides at its core an element which can only be described as hopeful. On the surface, we are more often out of step than in line with our animal, vegetable and mineral surroundings. The artist takes account of the complexity of experience and allows for our puzzlement, assuming optimistically that the things which bind us together are greater than the things that cleave us apart. If anything distinguishes the collective experience of being, it is the inevitability that mistakes will be made. Cross identifies a handful of these and shows us that in their contemplation lies the way forward. Forward to other mistakes, but forward nonetheless.

Paul Bonaventura

Erna Plachte Senior Research Fellow in Fine Art Studies

University of Oxford

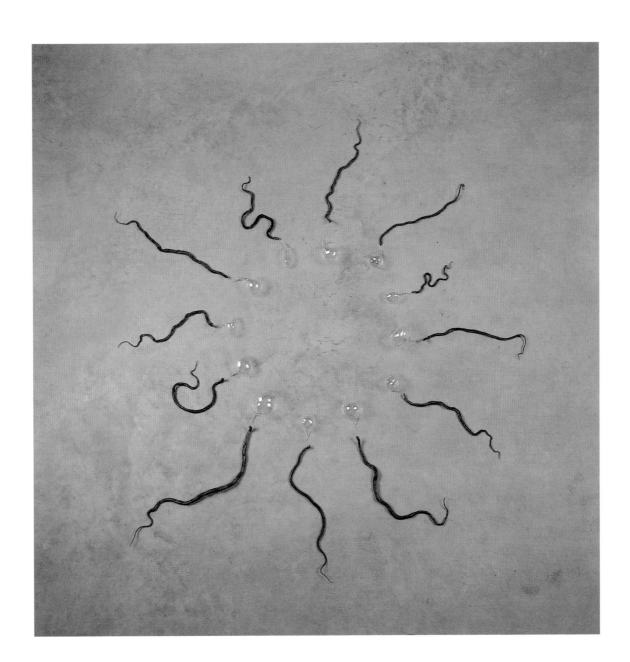

Convention 1995

Temptations urge you to force time – to take, to flee, to say before the time is right.

Mary Magdalene went alone to the tomb, or she went there with the other Marys. Whatever she sought there, in a place where a great stone was meant to block the entry to the tomb, what she found was a surprise. Where the body was supposes to be secure was an empty chamber, the entry gaping. Her shock was eloquent – and then words came, the first torrent which rushed in to take the place of the poor body.

What's up? she asked the loitering gardener, and when he tuned and spoke to her by name, Mary, she knew that despite appearances, this was no gardener. This was the invincible spirit of her hero in another shape. She rushed back to tell the others, and got things going. The body was gone, and into the momentary vacuum sped words, the Word perhaps, which last forever have no last at all.

It became the new, irresistible temptation, and the most unlikely betrayal – to abandon the flesh, the taste, to scorn the sight and quell the sound. *Touch me not, for I am changed and am of the word,* not world. It was another temptation to undo the first one, in which the counsel of the snake led to the biting of the apple of good and evil. That had cast them first into their bodies alone, ashamed, in a confusion of language burdened with procreation. After Mary Magdalene's little interview you are at it again, in reverse, waiting for the complex hollowness of words to work their wonders.

Wonders! The book has the authority of a ghost. One testimony becomes everybody's law, and considerable art seems like the anonymous transcriptions of a god; so Paul and Augustine work transformations on poor Jesus. Wonders numberless! At the hidden heart of the book there is a hole, and the absence is called spirit: it is the sign of something which is gone, for which symbols and substitutions multiply, numberless.

It is a book, because there is a hole in it. The hole is the guarantee that it all came about at the dictation of the spirit – which holds all these little letters, complaints and case histories together, the editor who is known but not seen. The hole is the empty tomb, the presence of that old temptation; it is one hundred gods made into one, illustrated by the same hand in one hundred faces, hands. More staunch than binding, more cool than representation, more confident than any picture: arrogant, the hole makes whole, the hollow is the real meaning.

The Jews would tolerate no images of their god. Who knows, anyway, in what shape a message or messenger appears? After the tomb showed its hollowness, the hero of the book is said to have turned up in many guises: a gardener, a shrouded man in the road, others. In each form an obsession with denial, and plenty of surprises: but recognisable, nonetheless, by the betrayal body, the eyes which know you, the big sounding hollowness that cuts through years, stories, as deep as can be.

James Conway

James Conway is a writer and opera producer working in Dublin

Bible 1995

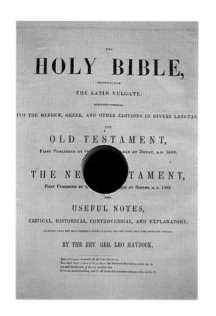

ABRAHAM'S SACRIFICE

NOAH PREPARING TO ENTER THE ARK

THE FINDING OF MOSES.

ELI AND SAMUEL.

CHRIST IN THE GARDEN OF GETHSEMANE

JACOB'S DREAM.

THE GOOD SAMARITAN.

THE PRODIGAL'S RETURN.

"Pandora replaced the lid. The box was almost empty, everything that was cruel, violent or swift had left it. All that was left, right at the bottom was a little thing which did not take up much space. It did not leap out like the others but was calm and assured. It was hope. It remained in the box as if afraid, as if it had not right to spread."[1]

The half open box arouses curiosity. It invites the viewer to participate in its mystery, to investigate its contents. While doing so is the viewer being viewed? Once engaged, something is revealed in an instant. Shocked, made curious, some linger to savour the erotic or retreat from the shame of self-pleasuring the intimacy of the contents, or recoil from the disgust of that which is hidden and repudiated, or pause to recognise a truth revealed within the taboo. I overheard an elderly woman say, as she lifted her head out of the box, "well, that's life".

The fact that these knickers lie hidden at the bottom of the trunk points to their potency. For whom and from what are they hidden? What power might be unleashed by possession. With the opening of Pandora's box, when, it was said, all the ills and spites were released into the world, Pandora was held responsible.

What is it about these knickers, with the cow's teat sewn into the gusset, that elicit such primitive and powerful reactions? The knickers contain the male and female parts – the udder that is phallus. For the infant the breast belongs to mother. She is the all-powerful, satisfying breast, that feeds, comforts and pleasures. Correspondingly, she can be the omnipotent bad breast that withholds food and comfort. As well as possessing the breast, in the infant's fantasy mother contains the father's penis inside her body. It seems to the infant that mother has everything. She possesses all that is desirable. So the infant is left without, in the position of longing, envy and desire. From this position of helplessness, the infant chooses to become the desired object of mother's desire, that is the phallus. The infant identifies with the phallus and wishes to possess it for mother. So the infant's desire and the desired object of mother's desire become interwoven.

The question remains does one ever succeed in fully relinquishing this desire and move on towards a desiring of one's own desire? And do these knickers with the phallic udder evoke a response that reveals more to us about our own viewing, than about that which we are engaged in viewing?

Marian Dunlea

Marian Dunlea is a psychoanalytic psychotherapist who lives in Dublin

1   F Comte, *Mythology – Compact Reference*, Chambers, 1991

Trunk 1995

I asked him if he would like to contribute to this book. If he would, he should tell me a story and, if he would allow me to make a suggestion, it should be our kind of story, in which you thrash about in the dark for a week or a month, it seems that it will be dark forever, and you feel like throwing it all up and changing your trade; then in the dark you espy a glimmer, proceed groping in that direction, and the light grows, and finally order follows chaos. Cerrato said seriously that indeed sometimes things went like that, and that he would try to come up with something, but in general it was really dark all the time. You couldn't see the glimmer, you beat your head again and again against an ever lower ceiling, and ended by coming out of the cave on your hands and knees and backward, a little older than when you went in. While he was interrogating his memory, his gaze fixed on the restaurant's presumptuously frescoed ceiling, I took a quick glance at him and saw that he had aged well, without deformations, on the contrary growing and maturing: he had remained heavy, as in the past, incapable of the refreshment of malice and laughter, but this was no longer offensive, and more acceptable in a fifty-year-old than in a youth of twenty. He told me a story of silver.

Extract from *The Periodic Table* by Primo Levi, pp203/204 (Published by Penguin Group)

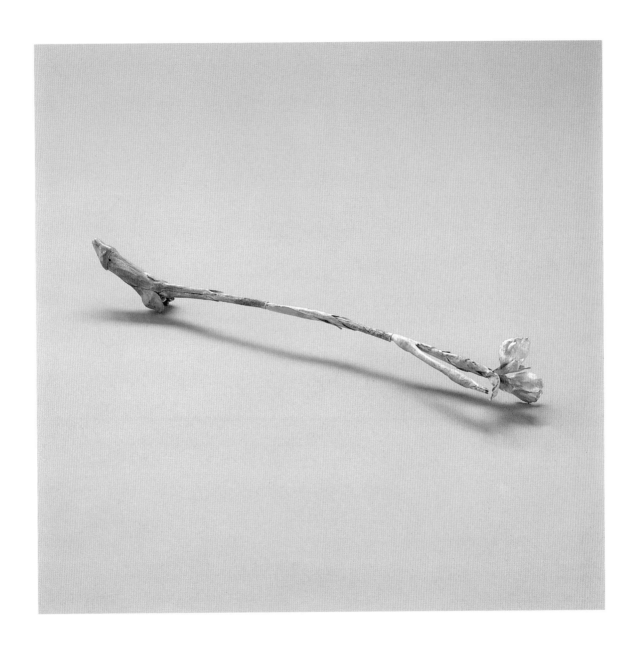

Iris 1994/95

"The usual stratagems and repositionings have failed to induce narcosis in me, so I decide to settle myself against the soft zigzag of her body. As I move and start to nestle my shin against a calf whose muscles are loosened by sleep she senses what I'm doing, and without waking reaches up with her left hand and pulls the hair off her shoulders onto the top of her head, leaving me her bare nape to nestle in. Each time she does this I feel a shudder of love at the exactness of this sleeping courtesy. My eyes prickle with tears, and I have to stop myself from waking her up to remind her of my love. At that moment, unconsciously, she's touched some secret fulcrum of my feelings for her. She doesn't know, of course: I've never told her of this tiny, precise pleasure of the night. Though I'm telling her now, I suppose …

"You think she's really awake when she does it? I suppose it could sound like a conscious courtesy – an agreeable gesture, but hardly one denoting that love has roots below the gum of consciousness. You're right to be sceptical: we should be indulgent only to a certain point with lovers, whose vanities rival those of politicians. Still, I can offer further proof. Her hair falls, you see, to her shoulders. But a few years ago, when they promised us the summer heat would last for months, she had it cut short. Her nape was bare for kissing all day long. And in the dark, when we lay beneath a single sheet and I gave off a Calabrian sweat, when the middle stretch of the night was shorter but still hard to get through – then, as I turned towards that loose S beside me, she would, with a soft murmur, try to lift the lost hair from the back of her neck".

Extract from *A History of the World in 10½ Chapters* by Julian Barnes, p226 (Published by Picador)

Lover Snakes 1995

Nemesis fled to the ends of the earth to escape Zeus, transforming herself into one animal after another, just as the manifest flees and scatters before being caught and pinned down by its principle. The same sequence of flight with metamorphoses followed by rape is repeated when Peleus chases Thetis and finally couples with her in the form of a cuttlefish. The repetition of a mythical event, with its play of variations, tells us that something remote is beckoning to us. There is no such thing as the isolated mythical event, just as there is no such thing as the isolated word. Myth, like language, gives all of itself in each of its fragments. When a myth brings into play repetition and variants, the skeleton of the system emerges for a while, the latent order, covered in seaweed.

Extract from *The Marriage of Cadmus and Harmony* by Roberto Calasso
(Published by Alfred A Knopf, Inc, 1993; published in Britain by Jonathan Cape Ltd, 1993, p136)

Cuttlefish Rings 1995

Untitled 1995

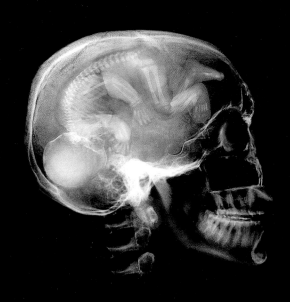

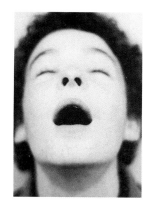   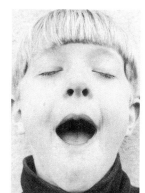

CLOSE YOUR

EYES AND

OPEN YOUR

MOUTH AND

SEE WHAT GOD

WILL GIVE YOU

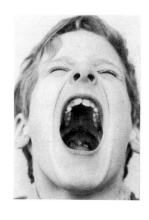 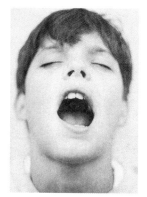 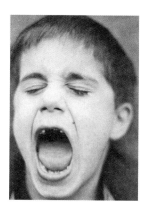

 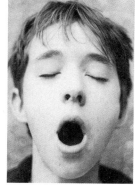 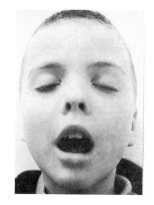 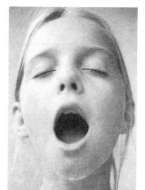

Crucifix 1996

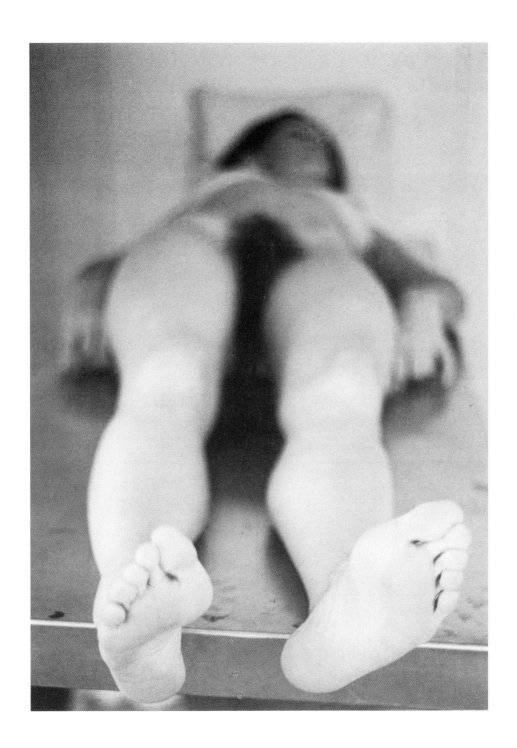

Mantegna 1995

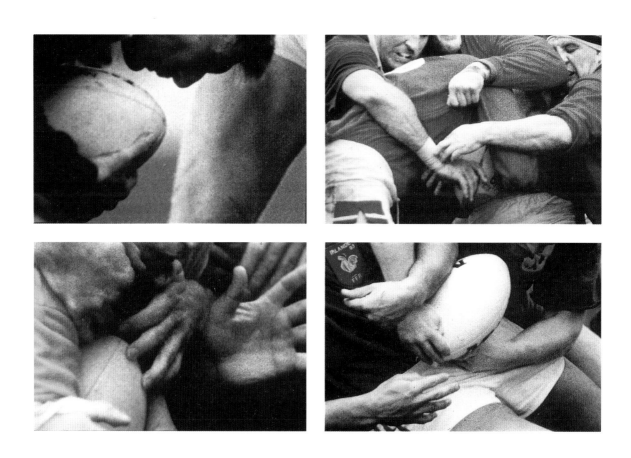

Rugby 1995/96

Croquet 1994

Rings 1995

Gallows 1995/96

biography

Dorothy Cross was born in Cork, Ireland in 1956. She now lives and works in Dublin.

Art Education

1973 – 1974	Crawford Municipal School of Art, Cork
19974 – 1977	Leicester Polytechnic, England (B.A. Degree)
1980 – 1982	San Francisco Art Institute, California (M.F.A. Degree)

Awards

1984, 1985, 1986	Arts Council bursaries
1988	P.S.I. Studio Scholarship, New York
1990	E.V.A. Open Award, Limerick
	Marten Toonder Award, Ireland
	Pollock Krasner Award, New York
1991	Arts Council bursary
	O'Malley Award, Irish American Cultural Institute
1992	E.V.A. Open Award, Limerick

One person shows

1980 and 1983	Triskel Art Centre, Cork
1984	Hendriks Gallery, Dublin
1988	Douglas Hyde Gallery, Trinity College, Dublin. *Ebb*
	Octagon Gallery, Belfast
1990	Kerlin Gallery, Dublin
1991	I.C.A. Philadelphia, USA. *Power House*
1993	Camden Arts Centre, London. *Parthenon*
	Douglas Hyde Gallery, Trinity College, Dublin (works from *Power House*)
1994	Kerlin Gallery, Dublin
	Frith Street Gallery, London. *Croquet*
1995	P.P.O.W., New York
	Kerlin Gallery, Dublin
1996	Arnolfini, Bristol. *even*

Selected group shows

1979/81	Diego Rivera Gallery, San Francisco, California
1982	Emmanuel Walter Gallery, San Francisco, California
1984	Hendriks Gallery, Dublin (4 gallery artists)
	Living Art Exhibition, Dublin (*Coronation Chair*)
1985	*Sculpture in the Chair*, Smiths Gallery, London
1986	G.P.A. Emerging Artists Exhibition, R.H.A. Gallery, Dublin
	Volm, Tokyo
1987	SADE, Crawford Gallery, Cork
1988	*A Sense of Place*, Battersea Arts Centre, London
1989	*Eclipse*, P.S.I. Institute of Contemporary Art, New York
	Open Studios, P.S.I., New York
1990	E.V.A., Limerick City Gallery
	Volm, Tokyo, Japan
	Irish Art of the Eighties, Douglas Hyde Gallery, Dublin
	Artpark, Lewiston, New York. Project – *Slippery-Slope*
1991	*Strongholds*, Tate Gallery, Liverpool and Sara Hilden Museum, Tampere, Finland
	E.V.A., Limerick City Gallery
	In a State, Kilmainham Gaol, Dublin
	Inheritance and Transformation, Irish Museum of Modern Art, Dublin
	The Fifth Provence, Contemporary Art from Ireland, Edmonton Gallery, Canada
1992	E.V.A., Limerick City Gallery
	EDGE Biennale, London and Madrid
	Erotiques, A.B. Galeries, Paris
	Welcome Europe, Holstebro Kunstmuseum, Jutland
1993	Kerlin Gallery, Dublin (Cross, Kindness, Prendergast)
	Other Borders, Grey Gallery, New York. Six Irish Projects,
	Venice Biennale – *An Irish Presence*
	Artscape Nordland – permanent work. *Shark. Cow. Bath*, Somna Kommune, Norway
1994	*Bad Girls,* I.C.A., London and C.C.A., Glasgow
	E.V.A., Limerick City Gallery
	Art-Union-Europe, Athens/Thessalonika/ Corfu
	Dialogue with the Other, Kunsthallen Brandts Klaedefabrik, Odense, Denmark/ Norrkopings Konstmuseum, Sweden

1995	*Beyond the Pale*, Irish Museum of Modern Art, Dublin
	Glen Dimplex Award Show, Irish Museum of Modern Art, Dublin
	Fetishism (organised by the South Bank Centre, London). Brighton Museum and Art Gallery, Castle Museum, Nottingham, Sainsbury Centre for Visual Arts, Norwich
	Frith Street Gallery, London
1996	E.V.A. Limerick
	Home and Away, Liverpool Tate
	Side Tracking, train project, Brussels

Publications

1991	*Sex and Death* – guest editor New *Observations* magazine, New York. Issue No 80
1993	Collaboration with Willie Doherty for cover of *Circa* magazine, Dublin. Issue No 64
1995	Collaboration with Loring McAlpin for cover of *Art in General* annual book, New York

Opera

1992	Set and costume design for Opera Theatre Company's production of *Tamberlane* by Handel. Kilmainham Gaol, Dublin; Theatre Royal, Wexford; Cork Opera House; St Columbs Theatre, Derry; Siamse Tire, Tralee
1994	Design for Opera Theatre Company's production of *Songs of Poems of Emily Dickenson* (Coplans) and *Diary Extracts of Virginia Wolfe* (Argento). The John Field Room, National Concert Hall, Dublin

Bibliography

1987	*Irish Women Artists*, The National Gallery of Ireland and the Douglas Hyde Gallery, Dublin. Exhibition catalogue with text by Aidan Dunne, John Hutchinson and Joan Fowler
1988	*Ebb*, Douglas Hyde Gallery, Dublin. Catalogue essay by Joan Fowler
1991	*Strongholds*, New Art from Ireland, Tate Gallery, Liverpool and Sara Hilden Museum, Finland. Catalogue with text by Penelope Curtis

	A New Tradition, Irish Art of the Eighties. Essays by John Hutchinson, Joan Fowler, Aidan Dunne and Fintan O'Toole
	Power House, I.C.A. Philadelphia, USA. Exhibition catalogue with essay by Melissa Feldman
	The Fifth Provence, the Edmonton Art Gallery, Canada. Essays by Elizabeth Kidd, Joan Fowler, John Hutchinson and Jamshid Mirfenderesky
1992	*Welcome Europe*, European art 1992. Catalogue for all E.E.C. countries. Essays in Irish section by Jesper Knudsen and Caoimhin MacGiolla Leith
1993	*Artforum* (May issue). Feature on Irish artists. Article by John Hutchinson
	Venice Biennale 1993 catalogue. Essay by Declan McGonagle
	Circa magazine No 64. *Irish Art in New York* by Anna O'Sullivan
	Sonsbeek, 1993. Catalogue, Arnhem
	Bad Girls, I.C.A., London. Catalogue with essay by Cherry Smyth
	Art in America, October. Lynn McCritichie (Three Installation Artists, News from London)
1994	*Art-Union-Europe*. Catalogue essay by Jaki Irvine
	Dialogue with the Other, Odense. Catalogue
	From Beyond the Pale, Irish Museum of Modern Art
	Art Monthly (September). Review of *Croquet*, Frith Street Gallery, London
1995	*Fetishism* – Visualising Power and Desire. Catalogue with essay by Roger Malbert
	Circa magazine No 72. Review of Glen Dimplex by Medb Ruane
	Irish Museum of Modern Art Glen Dimplex Artist Award catalogue
	Artforum (September). Review of P.P.O.W. exhibition, New York, by Ingrid Schaffner
	Kunstbeeld 9/95. Article by Rob Perée
	Laughter Ten Years After. Essay by Jo Anna Isaak
	Art in America, Dec. Article on Irish Art by Judith Higgins

list of works

1 *Rugby* 1995/96
   thirty cibachromes on MDF
   15¾in × 11¾in each

2 *Untitled* 1995
   black & white photograph, dry mounted on aluminium
   24in × 32in

3 *Cuttlefish Rings* 1995
   gold-plated silver, cuttlefish bones, glazed boxes
   12in × 16in × 2in

4 *Pointing the Finger* 1994
   cibachrome dry mounted on MDF
   14in × 14in
   photographs by John Kellet

5 *Trunk* 1995
   wood, cotton knickers, cow's teat
   40¾in × 23½in × 18in

6 *Bible* 1995
   wooden lap desk, bible
   22¼in × 17in × 14in

7 *Bandaged Snake* 1995
   snake, bandage, snake's heart in metal box
   25½in × 8in

8 *Lover Snakes* 1995
   snakes, silver reliquaries, hearts
   14¾in × 5½in

9 *Iris* 1994/95
   silver, wooden bench
   23½in × 3½in, Iris; 87in × 10¾in × 17¾in, bench
   lent by Hugh Lane Municipal Gallery of Modern Art,
   Dublin

10 *Convention* 1995
   twelve garter snakes, glass bubbles
   5in diameter

11 *"Close your eyes and open your mouth and see what God will give you"* 1995/96
   fifty black & white photographs
   15in × 20in

12 *Rings* 1995
   steel chains, bronze rings
   6½in diameter rings/chains variable

13 *Gallows* 1995/96
   snakes, rope, wood
   102in × 54in × 54in

14 *Mantegna* 1995
   black & white photograph on MDF
   photograph by Marych O'Sullivan
   Crucifix 1996
   cibachrome print on MDF
   photograph by John Kellet
   each 20in × 30in

15 *Goggles* 1995
   workman's goggles, wood, transparencies
   6½in × 3½in × 6½in

16 *Kiss* 1996
   plaster, electroformed in silver

All measurements length x height x depth

illustrated earlier works

p7 *Virgin Shroud* 1993
    cow hide, satin train, steel structure
    Collection: Tate Gallery, London

p8 *Stilettos* 1994
    shoes, cow's teats
    Collection: Marie and Joe Donnelly

p11 *Amazon* 1992
    cow hide, tailor's dummy
    Collection: Avril Giacobbi

p41 *Croquet* 1994
    croquet set, cows' udders
    Private collection, Ireland

acknowledgements

The artist would like to thank:

Tessa Jackson and Arnolfini for the invitation to show; my mother who continues to pass on family objects with curiosity, knowing that they will never be the same again; my father who gave me the things he found floating in the sea; James Conway and Marian Dunlea for their revelations; Paul Bonaventura for his essay and enthusiasm; Gerry McNamara who I miss for his rigorous wit and criticism; John Ronan for allowing me to work in his beautiful glass house over the river; the Irish Times Sports Department for letting me delve into their rugby files; the cows and snakes; the children who closed their eyes and opened their mouths and only got a packet of Rolos and my friends who kissed with mouths full of dental plaster.

Arnolfini would like to thank:

Paul Bonaventura for his illuminating text; James Conway and Marian Dunlea for their contributions which give learned insights from their own backgrounds; all the publishers who have given permission to use excerpts from their writers; Jimmie Durham for allowing us to use his poem; Frith Street Gallery, London in particular Jane Hamlyn and Rose Lord and John Kennedy and David Fitzgerald of Kerlin Gallery, Dublin who represent the artist; the Hugh Lane Municipal Gallery of Modern Art, Dublin who lent a work they had just acquired; colleagues at the other galleries where the show will be seen, and finally Dorothy Cross for her enthusiasm and way of looking at the world.

even

recent work by Dorothy Cross

is published by Arnolfini, Bristol
on the occasion of the following exhibitions:

24 February – 14 April 1996
Arnolfini
16 Narrow Quay
Bristol BS1 4QA
Telephone: 0117 929 9191
Facsimile: 0117 925 3876

18 May – 22 June 1996
Ikon Gallery
58–72 John Bright Street
Birmingham B1 1BN
Telephone: 0121 643 0708
Facsimile: 0121 643 2254

14 September – 26 October 1996
Oriel Mostyn
12 Vaughan Street
Llandudno LL30 1AB
Telephone: 01492 879201
Facsimile: 01492 878869

8 November – 21 December 1996
A selection of work will be shown at
Frith Street Gallery
59-60 Frith Street,
London W1V 5TA
Telephone: 0171 494 1550
Facsimile: 0171 287 3733

Organised by Tessa Jackson and Josephine Lanyon
Photographs by John Kellet, Dorothy Cross, Sarah Quick & James Woodley
Designed by Niall Allsop
Printed by Century Litho
Set in Gill Sans and Perpetua